Copyright
Copyright

# Press Release Power

How to write a Press Release for Online Distribution

Paul Clifford

# Contents

# Introduction

Everyone has heard of press releases. However not many people consider them for online exposure, traffic and for improving your search ranking – maybe because the costs are too prohibitive or because they don't have 'worthy' news?
Many people think that a press release can only be written and submitted by a PR professional.

In fact anyone can write a release for their business or website and publish to get attention.

That's not to say that this replaces the role of the PR consultant at all. Where the professional really adds value is to get your business in personal contact with the media. This can only be done effectively with the consultant's contacts in your specific business area, but of course there is a price for that.

I have written this with the smaller business in mind that doesn't necessarily have the wallet to fund large PR campaigns, but would like to see the benefits of attention and improvements in traffic to their business, that an online release provides.

I work for Ravepress (www.ravepress.com) which is an company that writes and distributes your press release on auto pilot and is designed for the small business with pricing to match. I have written this guide as a DIY manual using all the tips and tricks that Ravepress.com have used to enable their success. I hope you enjoy it and any feedback can be sent to me directly paul@ravepress.com.

# How To Write a Press Release for Online Distribution

The traditional way to get noticed in the press and online is to write and publish a press release and hope that it gets picked up and mentioned in a high volume newspaper or radio station. The other benefit which is equally important in today's online world, is if you get it posted correctly it will be syndicated to many websites who will backlink to your site and lift you up the rankings in the search engines.

Google and others see these links as high value as they are coming from official news sources. If your release is distributed correctly, Google will actually list them in its own news service guaranteeing you traffic as well. This will normally happen the day after you publish.

Many people tell me they don't know how to write a press release and many tell me they use a PR agency "for all that stuff". Well my answer to them is "Who knows the most about your product or service? - Yes you do" ...so who better to write it? Its really not that difficult and you just need to need to follow a formula.

# What To Write About?

Above all a press release has to be about something newsworthy. You have to be able to announce something, communicate a result, new win or something relevant to today's reader. You may think that you don't have much to say or there isn't anything new happening in your business that you would want to communicate. In fact if you put your mind to it, there's quite a lot you can write a release on.

Use the following list to gather ideas for new releases and plan a schedule over the course of the next 3 months (that's only 3 releases by the way) so you can start thinking about your monthly release cycle.

## Topics for Press Releases

Here are some angles for you to write releases about. They don't need to be dramatic but for great results, plan one a month.

### Your Products and Services

- New products or services.

- New or updated website

- Changes in pricing or special offers/discounts

- New releases of your products

- Different or new applications for your service or product

### Your Customers

- New contracts, wins and customers.

- Your customer success stories.

- Industry awards your customers may have achieved.

- Testimonials or recommendations received from customers.

### News and current topics.

- Write around and link with current news events.

- Pick on any statistics or surveys around your business area.

- Plan a networking event for your customers and communicate around that.

- Predict where you think your market is going.

- Link to something controversial or oppose a common belief

**Your Staff**

- New staff joining

- Industry awards or even your own awards won by employees.

- New training programs.

- Retirements.

**Marketing**

- Any exhibitions or trade shows you have been to.

- Perform a survey. (you can use surveymonkey.com)

- Publish a white paper

- Industry study

- Any public appearance or speaking engagements you or your staff have been involved with.

- Run a competition for an ipad or similar

**Your Business or Office.**

- Office move or expansion.

- An interview or meeting with a celebrity.

- Certification or awards of your business.

- Awards won by your organization.

- Industry associations you may have joined.

**Community Activities**

- Community sponsorship or activities

- Charities you may support

- Fund raising days you may be supporting

- Any of your staff performing something charitable

# The Structure of Press Release

What follows is a highly effective set of guidelines that will make your press release writing simple and straightforward. Just follow these simple rules:

A press release is formed of the following sections:

1) Headline
2) Subheadline or summary
3) Body
4) Company Information
5) Contact information

## 1) Headline

This is the attention grabber and must get readers attention, but more importantly, to be search engine optimized (SEO), it needs to have the primary keywords that you are trying to rank for in the title itself. It should be written in title case, that is each word should have a capitalized first letter.

You can rewrite any headline to make it more interesting and optimized for example (my keyword is 'kitchen cabinets':

Here is a stock headline:

*"Dertier offers new discounts on all kitchen cabinets stock"*

To be more interesting it can be re-written to be:

*"Kitchen Cabinets Store Dertier Cause A Stir With Massive Discount Sale"*

Your target keyword: "Kitchen Cabinets" is now at the beginning of the title – this enables it rank higher on Google for your target phrase and I think you'll agree it's a more livelier title.

## 2) Subheadline or summary

This should explain the headline but needs to be eye catching and interesting enough to ensure your reader will continue into the first paragraph of the body. This should be no more than 4 sentences and expand on your title and summarize the main message of your release.

3) Body

The first paragraph of the body should have the date a location specified as this:

*City, State / Country, date*

for example:

*Boston, MA, April 13, 2011 -*

This should then be followed by one paragraph about why this is interesting to your readers. It should also include your keywords that you are targeting.

The main content should follow and it should be based around the following principle…

- Who are you?
- What is the news?

- Where is it?
- Why is this relevant and interesting?
- How will your solution provide the benefit?

Keep your paragraphs clear, simple and easy to understand. The whole length of the body should be between 300-600 words.

Credibility factors in the body can be added by including a quote. You could either take a testimonial from your site, or even quote yourself.

## Call to Action
Include a sentence that asks the reader todo something. Don't leave it open ended. Remember the release has a purpose and you need to get your reader to your site. Use sentences like "for a free report on kitchen islands for the rich and famous visit "http://www.yoursite.com".

## 4) Your company information

This gives credibility. Its important to say what you do, how long you have been doing it and if possible how many customers you have or include any other measure of credibility you can think of.

This paragraph should only be 5 or 6 sentences long and should include a link to your website. The link should be clean (no embedding or anchor text) as the release may get printed.

## 5) Contact Information

Company Name

Contact Name

Address

Phone number

Email

Web address

Note it's important to ensure all of these fields are completed. Firstly a journalist might want to contact you, so you should make it as simple as possible for them get in touch. Secondly, it also tells the reader that you are a 'real' business and adds credibility.

# Advanced Strategies

How to supercharge your releases and deliver power to your marketing efforts.

## Multi-media

1)    Brand logos

Getting your brand image embedded in the release makes it eye catching and ensures that you'll get noticed above others.  It also adds to the credibility factor so essential on the Internet.

2)    Product images

Showing your products if at all possible adds substance to the news.  It helps the reader identify with what you are explaining and portrays a solid professional look to your news.

3)    Videos

Embedding videos is another way of showing your product or a way of getting your message across.  You can get the 'embed' code from your video and paste it into your news submission.

Click Share

then embed

Copy and
Paste this

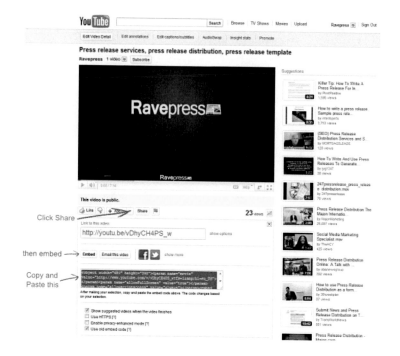

# THE MODERN PRESS RELEASE:

## Vegan Recipe For Caramel Corn At VeganCooking.com Advocates Yummy, Tasty And Healthy Eating

Attention grabbing headline

Share |

Social sharing tools

The well-known blog for vegan recipes, VeganCooking.com introduces the newest lip-smacking recipe for an all-time favorite movie snack Caramel Corn – vegan-style.

Orangeville, ON (I-Newswire) May 16, 2011 -
Lately, vegan diets and lifestyle have become extremely popular. Now more than ever, more people have embraced the practices of eating plant-based food and clearing the table from any meat, eggs, milk and honey products. While some people associate vegan food with unsavory dishes, vegans have come to innovate certain vegan recipes.

SEO Anchor text Link

A blog dedicated to sharing vegan recipes is VeganCooking.com. It is maintained by Claire Gosse, who also authors "Are You Sure That's Vegan?", a book that shows its readers how to produce vegan clones of their favorite breakfasts and deserts. The Ontario, Canada-based author started off by modifying recipes she had always used; utilized more of the meat alternatives that came on the market; and created VeganCooking.com to showcase them.

Interesting image - Grabs the eye straightaway

Continuously innovating vegan recipe discoveries, VeganCooking.com has just released the vegan version of the favorite snack: caramel corn. A healthier option than the basic popcorn, the vegan caramel corn is expected to be a perfect indulgence for the summer movie season that is soon to be in full swing.

Brandon Smiths enthuses about the vegan caramel corn: "I made this earlier this afternoon and it is awesome. Thanks for the great recipe."

Like other vegans, Mrs. Gosse rests on the fact that a vegan diet meets healthy eating necessities such as more vegetable, fruit or whole grain intake, thereby consuming more vitamins and minerals and decreasing saturated fat and cholesterol levels in the body. Studies also claim that well-planned vegan recipes can be suitable for diverse body and age groups.

Vegans are also generally known to exhibit compassion to animals with their plant-based eating practice. As animal lovers, Mrs. Gosse and her husband keep four dogs and three cats, and she volunteers her time at the local Ontario Society for the Prevention of Cruelty to Animals or OSPCA.

SEO Optimized links
Vegans and health-conscious individuals who want delectable food recipes can turn to http://www.vegancooking.com for easy-to-make healthy counterparts.

Embedded Youtube Video

**Additional Images**

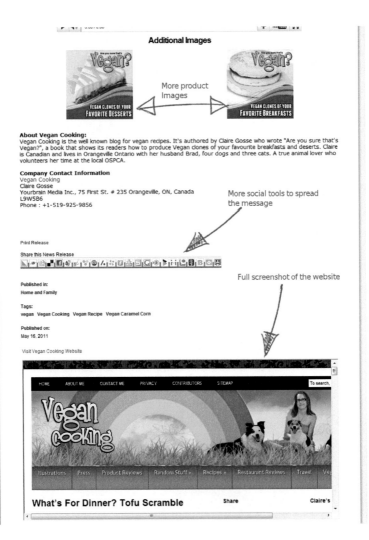

**Additional Images**

More product Images

**About Vegan Cooking:**
Vegan Cooking is the well known blog for vegan recipes. It's authored by Claire Gosse who wrote "Are you sure that's Vegan?", a book that shows its readers how to produce Vegan clones of your favourite breakfasts and deserts. Claire is Canadian and lives in Orangeville Ontario with her husband Brad, four dogs and three cats. A true animal lover who volunteers her time at the local OSPCA.

**Company Contact Information**
Vegan Cooking
Claire Gosse
Yourbrain Media Inc., 75 First St. # 235 Orangeville, ON, Canada
L9W5B6
Phone : +1-519-925-9856

More social tools to spread the message

Print Release

Share this News Release

Full screenshot of the website

Published in:
Home and Family

Tags:
vegan  Vegan Cooking  Vegan Recipe  Vegan Caramel Corn

Published on:
May 16, 2011

Visit Vegan Cooking Website

HOME  ABOUT ME  CONTACT ME  PRIVACY  CONTRIBUTORS  SITEMAP  To search,

Illustrations  Press  Product Reviews  Random Stuff »  Recipes »  Restaurant Reviews  Travel  Veg

What's For Dinner? Tofu Scramble  Share  Claire's

# SEO Aspects Of Your Release.

There are 3 main benefits to a press release. 1) Media interest and attention to your site, 2) The traffic this produces and 3) The benefits in search rankings.

Search rankings come from the a) the way your page is optimised for your target keyword and b) the number and quality of links there are to the sites.

**Headline Keyword.**
Always ensure your keyword is at the start of your headline. Google and other search engines will index based on this – and this is where the traffic will come from.

**Embed links into the text.**
A good press release distributor will allow you to embed up to 3 links into your text. The links should have anchor text so that the search engines understand what the link is about.

This is a link: http://www.mysite.com/excellent-product

This is a link with anchor text:

<a href="http://www.mysite.com/excellent-product">**My Excellent Product**</a>

Embedded within a paragraph all you would see is "My Excellent Product", but it tells the search engine what the target of the link is – which in turn increases your ranking for the phrase.

## 1st Link Counts

This is one of the most overlooked factors in search engine optimization. When Google scans a page for links – it will find a link to a destination page and examine that link for anchor text and all the other signals in its algorithm. When it finds the next link, if it goes to the same page, it will be ignored.

To illustrate this through example:

Lets assume a web page has the following links in it.

Link A: www.yahoo.com/page1  Anchor Text: "A great Page"

Link B: www.yahoo.com/page1  Anchor Text: "This is nonsense"

Link B anchor text "This is nonsense" will get ignored.

If however the links were the following:

Link A: www.yahoo.com/page1  Anchor Text: "A great Page"

Link B: www.yahoo.com/**a-nonsense-page**   Anchor Text: "This is nonsense"

Then link B would be counted and get the benefits of the algorithm.

When you are optimizing for a press release you should expect to have at least 3 anchor text link opportunities in your submission. You can see that it is fruitless to create 3 different anchortexts back to the same url.  Therefore create 1 for your home page, the second for a category page and a third for another page on your site that you're trying to promote.

When you do your subsequent press release then choose a different anchor text for each of those links.  (Its very important not to use one anchor text all the time – and you should mix it up with other similar words)

# How To Ensure You Benefit From The Panda Update.

The Google panda update is a new version of Google's algorithm that is designed to avoid poor content reaching the top pages of search results. Poor content is identified in many ways but most obviously it should not be copied from somewhere else on the web.

When designing the algorithm Google wanted to detect signals that a user might interpret as poor quality. Naturally their algorithm is confidential – but according to their feedback (extracted from the Google Webmaster Blog), the questions they are dealing with algorithmically are like these:

> Would you trust the information presented in this article?
> Is this article written by an expert or enthusiast who knows the topic well, or is it more shallow in nature?
> Does the site have duplicate, overlapping, or redundant articles on the same or similar topics with slightly different keyword variations?

Would you be comfortable giving your credit card information to this site?

Does this article have spelling, stylistic, or factual errors?

Are the topics driven by genuine interests of readers of the site, or does the site generate content by attempting to guess what might rank well in search engines?

Does the article provide original content or information, original reporting, original research, or original analysis?

Does the page provide substantial value when compared to other pages in search results?

How much quality control is done on content?

Does the article describe both sides of a story?

Is the site a recognized authority on its topic?

Is the content mass-produced by or outsourced to a large number of creators, or spread across a large network of sites, so that individual pages or sites don't get as much attention or care?

Was the article edited well, or does it appear sloppy or hastily produced?

For a health related query, would you trust information from this site?

Would you recognize this site as an authoritative source when mentioned by name?

Does this article provide a complete or comprehensive description of the topic?

Does this article contain insightful analysis or interesting information that is beyond obvious?

Is this the sort of page you'd want to bookmark, share with a friend, or recommend?

Does this article have an excessive amount of ads that distract from or interfere with the main content?

Would you expect to see this article in a printed magazine, encyclopedia or book?

Are the articles short, unsubstantial, or otherwise lacking in helpful specifics?

Are the pages produced with great care and attention to detail vs. less attention to detail?

Would users complain when they see pages from this site?

The most obvious and worst thing you can do is copy or duplicate content as its the easiest thing to detect on a search engine and it (the search engine) will always rank the original content higher.

**What this means for you** – is that its very important that your press release is published on your website first. That way Google will see you as the source of quality content and not the one of the press outlets.

## How do I do this?

The key is not only publishing it on your site.. but ensuring its indexed before you send out your release. The way todo this is to publish in the normal way through an html page or blog post and then ping the post. Most wordpress users will be familiar with this as it will normally do it for you. However if not this is the manual method.

1) Take the URL of your published press release.

2) Goto http://pingomatic.com

3) And submit your URL here as in the diagram:

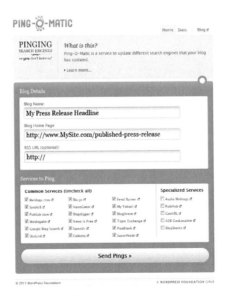

Will writing press releases hurt my site?
The Panda update is designed to lower the rankings of the

**publishers** of poor quality content, not the sites where any links

are pointing to. So as long as you are not publishing duplicated

releases then it will not effect your site.

# Hooks And Going Viral

To really get media attention and get the release syndicated – it has to have a headline that gets read.

To get it read – it has to have a hook or capture attention in a way that leads the reader to continue reading and then feel compelled to think 'yes!…that's an interesting story'.

How do you get your headlines interesting?
Firstly you can add drama, intrigue and a little trickery to catch the eye.

Example 1:  Using the kitchen island store example consider this headline:

*"Kitchen Island Mystery Revealed: How Butcher Block Tops Are Storming Everyones Kitchen"*

Its interesting and mysterious enough to lead in the reader to the rest of the story.

How about this example:

**"Kitchen Island Cover Up: The 1 Secret Of Butcher Block Tops They Don't Want You To Know"**

You may think – this is deceptive and how would you follow up on this. Well using a boring example of butchers block tops I could on to say how in fact butcher blocks actually have natural antiseptic properties in the wood and in tests plastic chopping boards actually contain more bacteria.

Yes its actually true… but the point of the example is you can make pretty mundane topics quite powerful. And the more its read, the more it will be syndicated and picked up by the press.

Another strategy is to link to something topical.

Find a fresh story or a big name that always gets news and link to it in this way:

**"Rachel Ray Move Aside: Real Cooks Use Kitchen Islands From Dertier.com"**

Another source of hooks is to create something interesting to discuss in your field. For example run a survey on your website for something contextual but slightly controversial.

For example (and following the kitchen islands idea.. again): Your survey could read like this:

How often do you scrub or wipe down your butchers blocks:

Hourly  - 1
Daily   - 2
Weekly – 3
Monthly - 4

After you've had a reasonable response, turn that into a story:
"Only 50% of households wipe or scrub down their butcher blocks – because they know they are hygienically protected by the wood"

# So I Have It Written What Now?

The next step is to submit your release to a PR distribution outlet. There are many to choose from and some even free but there are some important points you need to be wary of.

1) The free press release sites normally will not distribute and they will only publish on their own site.
2) Many paid services will take your release and distribute, but not give you benefits of SEO optimized anchor text links or video or images.

The best distribution networks are PR Newswire and PRWeb. Both of which will offer SEO optimized distribution for approximately $200/$300 upwards for each release.

If you want todo it for free, then select a number of free services and submit to each one individually.

The last alternative is to let Ravepress.com handle the whole process for you including optimization, images and videos. They will also submit to the top media outlets so your release will get the visibility it needs.

# Optimizing For The Search Engines

**Search engines, Google and why they all matter.**

The never-ending battle with search engines is the competition for the desktop. From the early days of Yahoo (previously the King of the search engine), to today, where the term "Google-it" is pretty much a household term.

There are many search engines available to users - but the primary ones are Google, Bing (previously Microsoft's MSN Search) and Yahoo. Google hold a 66% market share above Yahoo (17%) with Bing catching up (11%) to some degree due to some of its clever use of technology and slick interface.

With the search engines being the primary starting point for most household's quest for information - its essential that your company or website is listed as near to the top as possible. On most search result pages a list of websites will be displayed in what we call the "organic" section or the "paid for" section.

On Google for example the left hand side (except for the top 3 results highlighted in yellow) of the page is the organic section, and the right hand side is the paid for section.  In the Google world the technology that drives its  "paid for" listings is called adwords.

For anyone selling online however, when examining traffic – it's important to understand that organic results attract 90% of the clicks to a page as opposed to adwords which attract the remainder.  This is simply due to the fact that users try and avoid adverts as much as possible as they know they are being "sold to".

While its important to examine all the search engines, (you never know who will have market share in 5 years time) today Google dominates the search space and so for the remainder of this chapter we will focus on Google for search engine optimization (SEO)

SEO is the methodology we use to gain a position on Google in the organic listing section.  This position is called a SERP which stands for Search Engine Ranking Position.

## Traffic and keywords

Probably the most fundamental element of marketing online, especially with search engines is understanding keywords and commercial intent. A keyword or more accurately a "keyphrase" is the term that a user will type to find a specific result.

For example if I'm shopping for a coffee machine to make espresso - I might type "espresso coffee machine".

Commercial intent is the keywords ability to represent some one who is more likely to buy what you are selling. To demonstrate this in an obvious way look at these two keywords:

"espresso coffee machine"

and

"krups espresso coffee machine under $100"

Which one represents someone who is ready to buy do you think? Of course its the last one.

There is a trade off however with the longer keywords (we call these long-tail keywords) and that is for the number of searches of a primary keyword - there will a tiny number searches for long tail keywords, however there will be many more of them. The term "espresso" could produce many thousands of searches per day, but the long tail phrase above might only produce 5. The trade off is deepened when you understand that a tiny percentage of espresso searchers will turn into a sale - but large percentage of "krups expresso coffee machine under $100" will turn into a sale... assuming you sell it on your site of course. I'm sure by now you have realised that the key to success it getting your website position to appear for the right long tail searches... and for many of them.

## Understanding volumes and conversion

By now I hope you have started thinking about the types of words users might be entering to find your product, however here is the second fundamental concept in online marketing. Its called "find the traffic first."

So many people I speak to have setup a new business or ECommerce store, and have spent a ton on building the store - loading the products and launching their store only to find that their sales are much lower than expected. There may be many reasons for this - but the primary one is they don't research their market first. In any business you must establish that there is a **need** for something so you can be sure that there are people who will buy your product.

Online we look for traffic; volumes of searches for specific words that we believe will turn into sales. For example if I look at the volume of searches for "krups espresso coffee machine under $100" and I find there are 200 per day, I can assume that if my website was at the top of Google for that word then a certain percentage will visit my site (for example 50%) and of those visitors a certain amount will convert into a sale, lets say 1%, so 1 out of 100 visits to my site will buy my product. Thats a sale per day! Naturally the formula works on lower volumes too - if the search generated 20 searches per day - then this would product 1 sale every 10 days.

20 searches per day at 50% = 10 visitors per day.
Over 10 days = 100 visitors
1% conversion rate = 1 sale per 10 days

# Finding the words

The first place to look for keywords and the traffic itself is the
Google search engine.

Using this URL :

**https://adwords.google.co.uk/select/KeywordToolExternal**

You can login into the back office of Google itself and view the
traffic volumes for keywords.

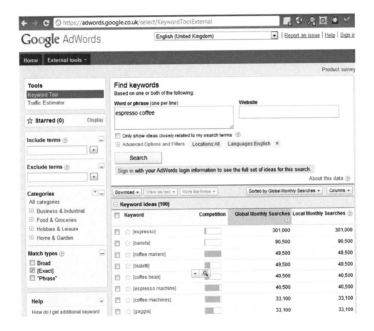

Lets start with "espresso coffee"

Enter that into the keyword box and click search and take a look at the results.

You will see many thousands of variants of the word together with the volume of searches for each. The variants will start to give you an idea of what people are actually searching for.

There are 3 types of keyword that Google presents to you: broad match, phrase match and exact match. In the left margin you will see the checkbox that allows you to select one or more of these options. When identifying which keywords to target, choose the exact match option. This give you the exact phrase together with the volume Google is estimating for the phrase. The volume is given as a monthly figure.

# Factors to consider when choosing your keywords.

## Volume

Putting effort into ranking a website for a certain term needs to be balanced with the volume that your site would attract when in position 1. The volume figure is the number of searches and not necessarily the number of clicks. The way to estimate the number of clicks your site is to take 40% of the volume figure. Working back from my conversion statistics above, if I want to make a sale per day then at 1% conversion rate I would need at least 100 clicks which at 40% of the searches means I need 250 searches per day. Using Google's figures I should be looking for words at around 7500 per month.

## Competition

Choosing the right search phrase is also dependent on the competition. If you choose a phrase that has been optimized for SEO over several years and has a team of 30 people ranking a site for that phrase, then naturally it will be tough for you to compete.

So how do you evaluate your chosen phrase for competition. Traditionally you would identify the number of pages in Google that mention your keyphrase. Nowadays its more appropriate to identify the number of pages with your keyphrase in the title of the page. You can use 2 queries for this:

1) put your keyphrase in quotes and search in Google and you'll see the number of results. "espresso machines" gave me "About 3,560,000 results" as the number of pages with a mention of the keyword in the page.

2) For the title you use the search phrase "intitle:"espresso machines"" and for me I got "About 1,720,000 results"

The last result tells me there are 1.7 million pages with "espresso machines" in the page title.

If you are new to SEO, to make a keyword rankable in a reasonable amount of time you should have the number of pages less than 100,000 and the number in title pages less than 50,000.

So it seems that "espresso machines" is too difficult to rank on. With this in mind I found a new keyword "krups espresso machine" which has 3,600 searches per month, less than 23,800 pages and 40,200 pages intitle. That's a worthy target phrase.

# Final competition analysis

To conclude the competitiveness analysis, search for your keyword and copy the top 5 URLs on the page into a text editor. Make a note of how many of the URLs have your keyword in the title of the page.

Then for the top 5 URLs search on "links:"url" in Google. This result will be the number of links that link back to the specific URL on the page. To outrank that page you would need to create more links than the ones ranking in the top 10.

Also note.. If the URL doesn't have the title in the page, then you would stand a good chance to outrank it.

If all this sounds a little complicated, there is an easier way and this it to download a tool called Traffic Travis which will perform all the keyword research automatically including showing you the statistics around competition. You can download it free of charge here **http://www.traffictravis.com/**

In summary you should now have a keyword that has:

1) Commercial intent
2) Suitable volume

3) Less than 100,000 competing pages and less than 50,000 pages with your search term in the title

4) Top 5 sites that have a low enough number of backlinks for you to beat.

# Onpage and Offpage SEO

These are two key terms that you will often hear and talk about in SEO. Onpage refers to any changes that you make to your website or web page to make it optimal for the keyphrase that you are targetting. Offpage refers to outside influences that effect he the ranking of your website, and most importantly the concept of external links to your site and the way they are constructed.

## Onpage in detail

Providing a web page to the user that ranks well is not as difficult as it might seem. In fact the offpage factors weigh in significantly more in terms of influence, but its essential to cover the bases with onpage. You need to ensure that the search engine has indexed your page in a way to make it decide to present your page higher than others. In doing so it is presenting the "most relevant" information to the user.

The factors to consider when doing this are the following:

**a) The Title**

The title of a webpage is the most important factor in a search engine deciding the relevancy of the webpage. It will look to whether the title matches the searched phrase or even a synonym of the search phrase - but either way it will decide and place the most emphasis on its decision based on your title.

The title of the page therefore must have the chosen keyphrase present and if you have more than one key phrase to target on a page then make sure your primary keyphrase is at the beginning of the title.

To show this in more detail using my example on the previous page - for "espresso coffee machine" the title could be:

Espresso Coffee Machine - The best choice online.

In the page html this would be written as

<title> = "Expresso Coffee Machine - The best choice online"

**b) The Header**

The header is a secondary method to describe the web page and is defined as the <h1>  This is usually shown and visible on the web page and represents the title of the content on the page.  It doesn't not need to match the keyphrase exactly - but it should at least contain the phrase in it.  For example

<h1> = "The best Espresso coffee machines online"

If you have any further subsections within your page - look to include similar words as the title of the subsection and put them in a <h2> section header.

## c) The description

The is the paragraph of text that's listed below the title in any search result.  Although Google doesn't actual index this - it will show it and highlight any of the keywords that the search finds in the paragraph.  This is also the opportunity to sell.  If you look at any search result you have 10-12 listings to select - what entices you to click on any of them?  This phrase can make or break the traffic that your website generates by enhancing the "click through rate" or CTR.

## d) The content

You should have at least 400 words of unique content on your page that has some relevance to the keywords that you are targetting. This doesn't mean repeat your keywords X many times so the text is unreadable. You should write for the reader and make it interesting and enticing for them to stay on the page. Plan to include your keyword at least twice and position at least the first mention of it within the first 100 words.

If you can insert images or videos into your content, but rename them to your keywords and include where possible alt text. Alt text is the way an image is described to the web browser, because the web cannot actually see an image. For example: ALT="Espresso Coffee Machine" tells the browser, and consequently the search engine that the image is an Espresso Coffee Machine. Naturally Google will include this in its list for relevancy.

# Uniqueness of content

The content must be unique as Google is focusing more and more on original content and treating this as a higher priority than other pages. The more unique and rich your page is the more likely it is to rank higher.  Google is trying to select and promote the original author of the content and so if you are using content that has already been indexed, then it won't promote your page as high as the original authors.

# Offpage Optimization

Google from its early days as "back rub" had its origins in the concept that when other sites link to your site - it must have something of value. This has expanded from the basis of the Google algorithm and combined with a concept called authority. Authority is the measure that Google places on a site and it scores this out of 10 (10 being the highest). Google keeps it authority score private but does publish a version of authority which it calls "page rank". Page Rank or PR is the public metric of the authority of a page. You can check the PR of a page by entering the URL into a site such as "checkmypagerank.com"

Today Google will rank your page depending on the number of links there are to it, the authority of those links and how those links are described. For example if I have a link from CNN or BBC, then this is a high authority link (with a PR of 9 or 10), and so Google will consider that my page must be of considerable value for the BBC to link to it. So any SEO's objective is to try and gather links of a higher PR.

You can now see that the way to get ranked is to get links, however there is a further element to understand and that is the concept of anchor text. In any link the anchor text describes what the link is about and potentially what the page is that its linking to.

The link would look like this:

<a href="http://www.mycoffeewebsite.com/">**Espresso coffee machines**</a>

the part in bold is the anchor text and describes the content.

## Quality and quantity of links

By now you can see the idea is to get lots of links to your page of high quality (or PR) and then your page will rank in Google. Whats important is to ensure that you don't create whole load of links overnight and make them all have the same anchor text. You see Google wants pages to collect links naturally and so if you are to replicate this then you would create a few links on a daily basis and make them from lots of different and unique sites varying the anchor text as well and quality of the sites. The volume of links you attract per day should be related the age of your site or domain.

You can read further on linkbuilding strategies, using a book called "The Art of SEO" by Rand Fishkin.

However, its key to understand that as part of your link acquisition strategy – publishing quality press releases is a formidable tool ranking your website.

# To Conclude

From this book you now understand how to write a press release for attention, how to optimize it for SEO and target it correctly, including submission.  Lastly you learnt how to choose the right keywords for your website and how to optimize your website to attract links from other sites including the media.

The key is to consistently publish releases once per month, which improves your traffic, and search engine visibility

# About Ravepress

Ravepress is an organization that simplifies press release writing and distribution. Designed specifically for Internet publishing, the company takes a short news summary from a business or website and writes a quality eye catching release. The user can then review and approve the release prior to it being distributed using the PR distribution network. A Ravepress release ends up on over 39 high quality US media outlets including Google News. This brings to the company backlinks, traffic and ultimately more sales. You can visit Ravepress here http://www.ravepress.com/

# Free Press Release Sites

http://www.betanews.com

http://www.directionsmag.com

http://news.thomasnet.com/

http://www.nanotech-now.com

http://www.prlog.org/

http://www.downloadjunction.com

http://www.newswiretoday.com/

http://www.pr-inside.com/

http://www.24-7pressrelease.com

http://www.pr.com/

http://www.prleap.com/

http://www.free-press-release.com/

http://www.clickpress.com/

http://www.pressbox.co.uk/

http://www.filecluster.com/

http://www.onlineprnews.com/

http://www.i-newswire.com/

http://www.cgidir.com/

http://www.przoom.com/

http://www.openpr.com/

http://www.sbwire.com/

http://www.1888pressrelease.com/

http://www.theopenpress.com/

http://www.free-press-release-center.info/

http://www.prfree.com/

http://www.ukprwire.com/

http://www.itbsoftware.com/

Made in the USA
San Bernardino, CA
04 March 2017